CONTENTS

KEEPING WARM

Do you feel hot or cold? How can you tell?
How can you make yourself warmer or cooler?
These are just three questions about keeping
warm. In science, people ask lots
of questions and find out the answers
by doing experiments. This book looks
at the essential facts about how
things warm up and cool down.

Measuring temperature

A thermometer is used to measure how
hot or cold something is. This is called
its temperature.

The thermometer tells you how
hot or cold something is.

A gas or wood fire can help to keep a room warm.

Where warmth comes from

Outside our homes the air and the ground
are warmed by the heat of the sun. Inside
buildings, a fire and radiators warm the
rooms. Warm food and drinks make us feel
warm, but most of our warmth comes from
our food in a different way. As our body uses
food to grow or to move about, this process
creates warmth. This warmth spreads round
our body in our blood and keeps us warm.

Essential Science ✔

ping
rm

Peter Riley

W
FRANKLIN WATTS

This edition 2010.

First published in 2006 by Franklin Watts
338 Euston Road, London NW1 3BH

Franklin Watts Australia
Hachette Children's Books
Level 17/207 Kent Street, Sydney NSW 2000

Editor: Rachel Tonkin
Designer: Proof Books
Picture researcher: Diana Morris
Illustrations: Ian Thompson

Picture credits:
Erik Aeder/Pacific Stock/Photolibrary: 19t; Jeremy Bishop/Science
Photo Library: 27cr; Martin Bond/Science Photo Library: 23tr; Bob
Daemmich/Image Works/Topfoto: 16c; Michael Kevin Daly/Corbis:
6bl; Dimplex: 10b, 28cr; Philippe Hays/Rex Features: 17t; Image Source/Rex
Features: 22br; David Hay Jones/Science Photo Library:
9cl; Magdalene Lindholm/Greatshots/Photolibrary: 15; Roel
Loopers/Photolibrary: 20c; Tony McConnell/Science Photo Library: 11b; Ariel
Skelley/Corbis: 11t. Trevor Smithers ARPS/Alamy: 22cl; Bob
Stelko/Botanica/Photolibrary: 7tr; David Taylor/Science Photo Library: 27tl;
Ian West/Photolibrary: 21tr; Stuart Westmorland/Corbis: 6tr;
Elizabeth Whiting & Associates/Corbis: 22-23; Roger ilmhurst/FLPA/
Corbis: 21cl, 29tr; Michael Wong/Corbis: 14, 29tl.

With thanks to our models: James Cook and Gloria Maddy

A CIP catalogue record for this book
is available from the British Library

ISBN 978 0 7496 9600 9
Dewey Classification: 536.5

Printed in Malaysia

Franklin Watts is a division of Hachette Children's Books,
an Hachette UK company.
www.hachette.co.uk

Warmth and heat

If you put your hands near a radiator you can feel heat coming from it and warming your hands. Heat can move about, but it moves through different materials at different speeds. Here's an easy experiment to find out how heat moves. Stand a plastic spoon and a metal spoon in a cup of hot water. After a few minutes the metal spoon will feel warmer than the plastic spoon because heat travels faster through metal than plastic.

The metal spoon feels hotter than the plastic spoon.

Materials which allow heat to pass through them quickly are called heat conductors. Materials which only allow heat to pass through them slowly are called insulators. Conductors and insulators can be used to control how heat moves.

Using data

When scientists do experiments they make observations, and then record them. This information is called data. It may be recorded in a table, bar chart or line graph. Collect some data about keeping warm by trying this activity. Make a list of all the things in your home that provide heat, then divide them into things that heat rooms, food, water and people, such as hot water bottles. Make the list into a bar chart like the one shown here. How does your data compare? All the answers to questions in this book are on page 31.

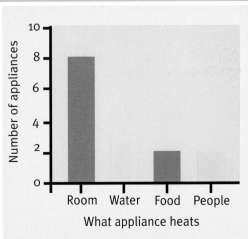

5

HEAT AND ENERGY

We all know that when we run around we get hot and sweaty, but why do you think this is? The answer is to do with energy.

The sun produces vast amounts of energy in the form of heat and light.

What is energy?

Has anyone ever asked you where you get all your energy from? Running – or any kind of movement – is a form of energy. Energy comes in lots of forms: for example movement, heat, light and sound. Another important fact about energy is that it can change from one form to another.

Where does energy come from?

The movement energy we create when we run ultimately comes from the sun through the energy it gives the plants we eat. In the centre of the sun, a gas called hydrogen is squashed together so much by the sun's gravity that it changes into another gas called helium. When this happens, energy is released from the gases and it escapes from the sun as heat and light.

You need plenty of energy to take part in a game like football.

How do we get energy from the sun?

Light energy from the sun is absorbed by the green leaves of plants. Plants use the energy to make food by using some common chemicals: hydrogen and oxygen from water, and carbon from carbon dioxide in the air. This process is called photosynthesis. It changes light energy into chemical energy which is stored in plants. When you eat plants you take in chemical energy. Humans eat plants in the form of fruit and vegetables, cereals and grain. In your muscles, the chemical energy changes to movement energy so you can run off and play a game.

The light energy absorbed by a banana tree's leaves is changed into chemical energy and stored in its fruit – the bananas.

You eat the banana which gives you energy to run around.

Looking for energy in food

Scientists measure the amount of chemical energy in food in units called kilojoules. The kilojoule symbol is kJ. Here are the energy measurements of 100 grammes (g) of some foods.

Divide the list into high-energy and low-energy foods. Look at the labels on packets and tins of food and find the amount of energy in them.

ENERGY in FOOD	
Food (100 g)	Energy (kJ)
spaghetti	1549
apple	197
orange	150
peanut	2428
chicken	736
milk	274
bread	1025
banana	326
jam	1116

TEMPERATURE

We can compare the temperatures
of different objects by simply touching
them if they are not too hot or too cold.
If we want to make an accurate
comparison of the temperatures
we use a thermometer.

C   F

Glass column

Alcohol

Scale in degrees Fahrenheit

Scale in degrees Celsius

Bulb

How does a thermometer work?

This thermometer is made from
a glass tube with a swelling
called a bulb at one end.
Inside the bulb and tube is a coloured
liquid called alcohol. When a substance is heated, it expands,
by how much depends on what it is. When the bulb is heated,
the glass expands a little and the alcohol expands a lot.
The expanding alcohol rises up the tube. The alcohol column
expands steadily as it gets warmer. This means that for a certain
rise in temperature the column of alcohol lengthens a certain
amount so it can be used as a measure of temperature.

Two scales of temperature

There are two scales of temperature used by scientists. They are the Celsius scale and the Fahrenheit scale. On the Celsius scale, water freezes at 0°C and boils at 100°C. On the Fahrenheit scale, water freezes at 32°F and boils at 212°F.

Some thermometers use electricity to measure temperature.

Using temperature readings

A healthy human body has a temperature of 37°C. If someone is ill their body temperature may be slightly higher or lower than this. Doctors and nurses check a patient's temperature to help them decide how to treat them. For example, if the temperature is higher than 37°C the patient may have a fever and they can be treated to lower their temperature.

Temperature is very important for many things. Scientists who study the weather take the temperature of the air in different places during the day and night. They use the measurements to make maps to show how cold and warm air move over the Earth. This helps them to predict the weather.

The thermometer at this weather station is shaded from the rays of the sun by a special cover called a Stevenson's screen.

Reading thermometers

Sometimes it is useful to draw diagrams of thermometers to record results.

What are the temperatures in degrees Celsius shown by these three thermometers?

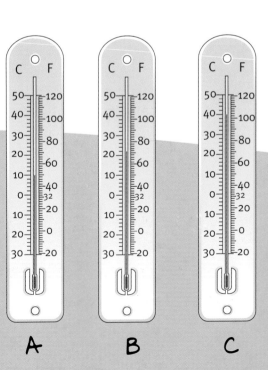

A   B   C

HOW HEAT MOVES

Heat always moves from a warm place to a cooler place. This is why your tongue feels cold when you lick something cold, such as an ice lolly. Heat can move in three different ways, depending on what it is moving through. The three ways are called conduction, convection and radiation.

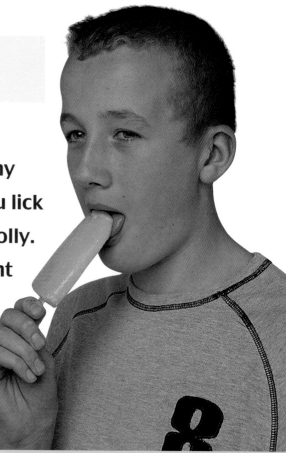

Heat passes from your tongue to the ice lolly by conduction.

Conduction

Heat moves by conduction when two things are touching and one is warmer than the other. When your tongue touches an ice lolly, the heat moves from it by conduction because it is warmer than the ice lolly. Conduction takes place mainly in solids.

Convection

Solids cannot flow but liquids, such as water, and gases, such as air, can. When they flow, they can carry heat with them. This flowing movement of heat is called convection.

A convection heater has holes in the top. When the air in the heater is heated by electricity, it flows out through the top and more cold air flows in at the bottom.

What is radiation?

Heat can also move in the form of rays, just like light does. You can see rays of light shine through a gap in your bedroom curtains in the morning. You cannot see heat rays but you can feel them. If you sit round a campfire, heat rays spread out from the fire and warm your face, hands and knees. Your back feels cold because the heat rays cannot bend and warm it. They move in straight lines like rays of light.

Radiation does not need a solid, liquid or gas to help it move heat like conduction and convection do. It can carry heat and light from the sun across empty space . If heat could not travel in this way, it would be too cold for life on Earth.

Heat rays spread out in all directions from a fire.

What does a thermograph show?

Special cameras can show the radiation of heat as a picture called a thermograph. The amount of radiating heat is shown by a colour ranging from blue (smallest amount) to green, red, yellow and white (largest amount). Which are the hottest and coolest parts of the object in this thermograph?

A thermograph of a teapot, cup and saucer.

CONDUCTORS AND INSULATORS

A conductor is something that allows heat to pass easily through it by conduction. An insulator is something that does not let heat pass easily through it.

How does heat pass through a solid?

When the spoon is put in a beaker of hot water, the part of the spoon in the water becomes hot as the heat from the water is transferred into it by conduction. The heat then passes up the spoon, transferring heat from the hot part to the cold part by conduction until eventually the whole spoon is hot.

Conduction of heat

Heat moves from one part of a spoon to another by conduction.

Good conductors

A good conductor allows heat to pass through it quickly. Metals are good conductors. Metals feel cold when you pick them up because heat from your hand moves through them quickly so they take more and more heat from your skin.

Poor conductors

A poor conductor is also called an insulator. An insulator does not allow heat to pass through it quickly. The heat moves very, very slowly so that you can almost think of insulators as materials that stop heat flowing. Wood, plastic, cork and cloth are insulators.

Conductors in the kitchen

Heat is needed to cook food. Pans are made from metals because they are good conductors so they can pass heat quickly from the oven to the food. Poor conductors such as plastic and wood are used to make pan handles so the heat from the metal in the pan cannot reach the cook's hands.

stainless steel

plastic

wood

cast iron

copper

Different kinds of metal are used to make pans. The handles are designed to stay cool.

Predicting a result

The data in the table shows how long it took for butter to melt when put on spoons made from different materials and placed in a cup of hot water. Which is the best conductor? Which is the best insulator?

Material	Time
copper spoon	5 seconds
plastic spoon	30 seconds
steel spoon	10 seconds
wooden spoon	50 seconds

BODY HEAT

When energy changes from one form to another, part of it always changes into heat. Your body gets the energy it needs from the food you eat. When the energy in food changes, some of it becomes heat, which warms your body.

Releasing the energy in food

The energy in food is stored energy. It is released from its store in your body by a process called respiration. In respiration, this stored energy and oxygen from the air take part in an irreversible change. One of the substances that is made in this change is carbon dioxide. This is a poison so the body gets rid of it by releasing it into the air when we breathe out. Water is also produced during respiration and this is released in our breath, sweat, and when we go to the toilet.

We take in oxygen for the respiration process when we breathe in and release carbon dioxide from the respiration process when we breathe out.

Energy in the body

When energy is released from food it can be used in many ways. It can be used for moving about or helping the body grow and repair any damage such as cuts and bruises. Some energy is used to help digest food, make the heart beat and keep the senses and brain working. Whenever the energy is changed for any of these purposes, some changes into heat energy.

Burning food

The process of respiration is a bit like food being burnt. If you think of food cooking on a barbecue, sometimes it catches fire. The energy in the food takes part in an irreversible change with oxygen in the air. The stored energy is released as heat and light in the form of flames. Carbon dioxide is also released. Respiration in the body works in a similar way but produces energy that helps us to move and keep us warm.

Heat and light energy are released from food when it burns.

Energy and activities

1 Which activity uses the least energy?

2 Which activity uses the most energy?

3 What link can you see between the activities and the amount of energy used?

4 Arrange the activities in order, starting with the one that uses the least energy.

Activity	Energy used per minute KJ/min
Cycling	27
Swimming	30
Sitting at computer	5
Soccer	36
Sleeping	3
Walking	17

SWEATING AND SHIVERING

If we get too hot we sweat. If we get too cold we shiver. Sweating and shivering help to keep our body's temperature at about 37°C. This is the temperature at which our body works best and is most healthy.

How does sweating cool us down

When we get too hot, sweat is released from our skin. Sweat is mainly water. The water takes up the heat in the skin by conduction which helps to cool us down. The heat makes the water in the sweat evaporate. Water changes into a gas called water vapour when it evaporates.

What happens if we get too hot?

In very hot weather, unless we avoid the heat, the body stops sweating and its temperature rises to 41°C. An illness called heat stroke may develop. A person suffering from heat stroke gets a headache, becomes sick and may then become unconscious and, in the worst case, die. Heat-stroke victims can be helped to recover by keeping them in the shade, cooling them with a fan and sprinkling slightly warm water on their skin.

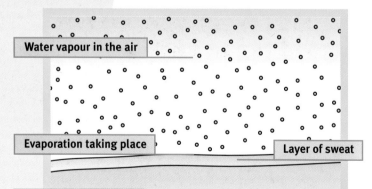

Water vapour in the air

Evaporation taking place

Layer of sweat

Heat from inside body

Water vapour takes the heat away from the skin into the air.

How does shivering warm us up?

Shivering is caused by short, rapid movements of the muscles. When we shiver, stored food energy in the muscles is changed to movement energy and some energy is released as heat.

What happens if we get too cold?

In very cold weather lots of heat can escape from our body and our temperature falls. This makes us shiver. If shivering doesn't warm us up enough, our body temperature falls lower and we might get a headache. If a person's body temperature falls below 26°C, they develop hypothermia and may become unconscious and die. A person suffering from hypothermia can be helped to recover by being wrapped in blankets. If they are conscious, they can be given a warm drink.

When people are rescued from cold water they may have to be treated for hypothermia.

Reading a clinical thermometer

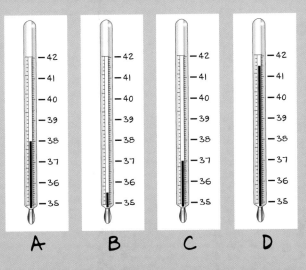

A   B   C   D

A clinical thermometer is used to read body temperature so its scale has a range of only a few degrees, usually 35°C to 42°C. Thermometer A shows a temperature of 38°C.

1 What temperature does each of the other thermometers show?

2 Which one shows the temperature of a person who may begin to suffer from hypothermia?

3 Which one shows the temperature of a person suffering from heat stroke?

WARM CLOTHES

Hold out your hand. What is it touching? You may say that it is not touching anything but you would be wrong. It is touching the air around it. If the air is cooler than your hand, heat will leave your hand by conduction then move through the air by convection.

Warm clothes form a barrier between our skin and the air.

Do warm clothes give us warmth?

Warm clothes simply stop the heat leaving our bodies quickly and so keep us warm. The heat comes from us.

Why are warm clothes thicker than other clothes?

Clothes are made from fibres. Fibres are solid threads and heat can pass through them by conduction. In warm clothes the fibres form a thick layer with air trapped between them. It is the air that traps the heat. It can pick up heat by conduction but it cannot carry it quickly by convection. Air is an insulator.

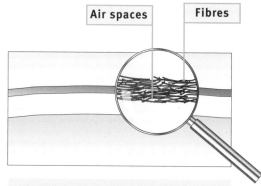

Air spaces | Fibres

The air trapped in the fibres forms a layer of insulation.

Why convection does not work

Air needs a large space, like a room, in which to flow. In warm clothes, the air is trapped in small spaces between the fibres and cannot flow anywhere. This means that it cannot carry heat away by convection.

Wet suits

Water in the sea, lakes and rivers is much colder than the body. People who take part in water sports, such as surfing or canoeing, wear wet suits. A wet suit is made from a material called neoprene. It is an insulator. The wet suit gets its name from the layer of water that is trapped between the neoprene and the skin. This acts as an insulator, too, like the layer of air in clothes worn on land.

Wet suits keep people warm who take part in water sports.

Comparing materials

Six cups were wrapped in materials A – F. Hot water was poured into each cup and the temperature of the water was taken at the beginning of the experiment and fifteen minutes later. The results were recorded in a table.

Material	Temperature at start (°C)	Temperature after 15 minutes (°C)
A	60	40
B	60	38
C	60	41
D	60	51
E	60	28
F	60	35

1 What was the drop in temperature in each cup?

2 Which material was the best insulator?

3 Which material was the best conductor of heat?

HOW ANIMALS KEEP WARM

There are two kinds of animals: cold-blooded animals and warm-blooded animals.
They both get energy from their food and some of it is released as heat in their bodies.

Cold-blooded animals

Cold-blooded animals, such as reptiles and insects, cannot control the temperature of their bodies. If their surroundings are warm, heat passes into them and they warm up. If their surroundings are cold, heat leaves their bodies and they cool down.

Some cold-blooded animals can help themselves to warm up. Insects, such as moths, can move their wing muscles quickly to create heat. Reptiles, such as snakes and crocodiles, bask in the sun's rays to warm up.

This crocodile is taking in heat radiating from the sun to warm itself up.

A crocodile's changing temperature.

Cold-blooded animals, such as the crocodile, do not have a set body temperature. On a cool day their body temperature will stay low but on a hot day their body temperature may rise as high as that of a warm-blooded animal.

How do warm-blooded animals stay warm?

Mammals and birds are warm blooded. Some mammals are covered in hair or fur, which traps an insulating layer of air. Some mammals, such as seals, which live in cold water, have an extra insulation layer of fat under their skins. The feathers covering a bird's body trap air like the hairs of a mammal. Humans are mammals but we do not have enough hair on our bodies to keep us warm. We wear clothes to keep warm instead. The first humans wore animal skins to keep warm.

Water evaporating from inside an open mouth helps animals cool down.

In cold weather a bird fluffs out its feather to make a thicker insulating layer of air.

When animals get too warm

Both cold-blooded and warm-blooded animals can get too warm if their surroundings are too hot. A crocodile gapes to let more heat escape from inside its mouth. Dogs are warm blooded and pant to let air from inside their bodies take heat away.

The temperatures of animals

1 Which animal has the widest range of body temperatures?
2 Which animals are warmer than humans?
3 Which animal can have the same temperature as a human?

The temperatures of animals (°C)	
Human	37
Dog	39
Pigeon	41
Lizard	31–35
Rattlesnake	12–37
Salmon	5–17

KEEPING HOMES WARM

Energy is needed to warm your home. You can save energy by making sure it is well insulated.

The stored energy in gas is changed to heat and light in a gas fire.

Home warmers

A home can be warmed by electricity or by fuels such as gas or oil. Heaters change electrical energy into heat and fires release the stored energy in fuels. If a home is well insulated, less electricity and fuel is needed to keep it warm. This helps save fuel, energy and money.

WALLS
Some heat can pass through air gaps called a wall cavity by convection.

Filling the cavity with foam stops the air flowing around the cavity and stops heat moving by convection.

Keeping the heat in

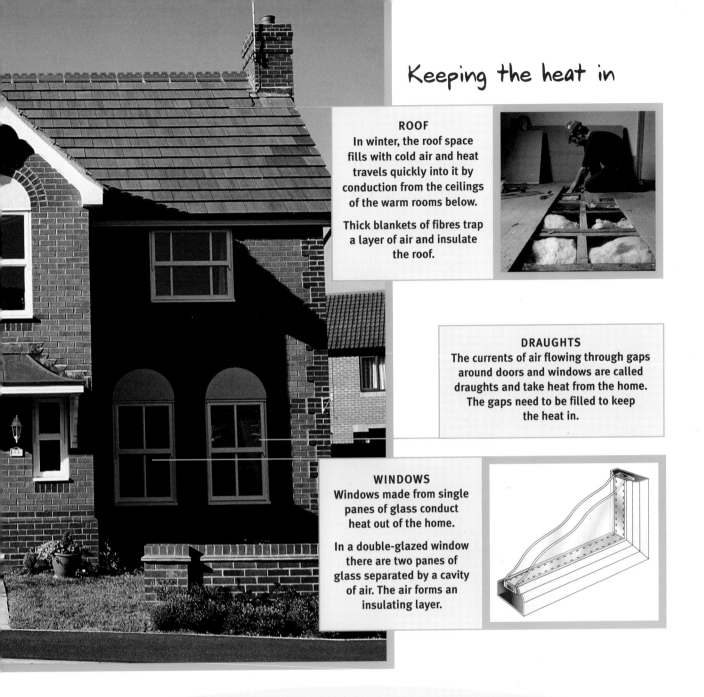

ROOF
In winter, the roof space fills with cold air and heat travels quickly into it by conduction from the ceilings of the warm rooms below.

Thick blankets of fibres trap a layer of air and insulate the roof.

DRAUGHTS
The currents of air flowing through gaps around doors and windows are called draughts and take heat from the home. The gaps need to be filled to keep the heat in.

WINDOWS
Windows made from single panes of glass conduct heat out of the home.

In a double-glazed window there are two panes of glass separated by a cavity of air. The air forms an insulating layer.

How much heat is saved?

How much heat is saved by
1 filling up gaps?
2 fitting double glazing?
3 filling wall cavities with insulation?
4 using insulation in the roof space?

Part of home	Heat lost without insulation	Heat lost with insulation
Gaps in doors and windows	15%	6%
Windows	10%	5%
Walls	35%	12%
Roof	25%	5%

THE THERMOS FLASK

You may use a thermos flask to keep drinks hot or cold when you go on a picnic.

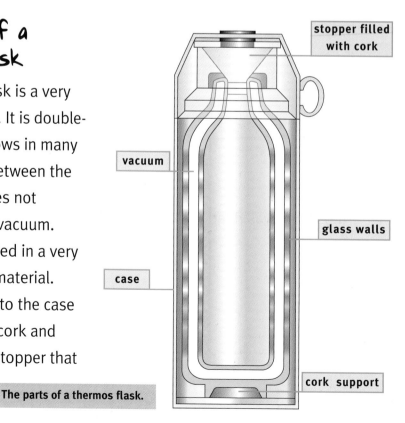

The parts of a thermos flask

Inside a thermos flask is a very unusual glass bottle. It is double-glazed like the windows in many homes but the gap between the two walls of glass does not contain any air. It is a vacuum. The walls are also coated in a very shiny silvery-coloured material. The bottle is connected to the case of the flask by pieces of cork and there is a cork or plastic stopper that fits in the top.

stopper filled with cork

vacuum

glass walls

case

cork support

The parts of a thermos flask.

How the flask works

When the flask is filled with a hot drink, heat tries to escape but the way is almost completely blocked. Glass is a poor conductor of heat so the heat travels slowly through the first wall of the bottle. When heat reaches the shiny surface, only a tiny amount of heat leaves by radiation. This is because shiny surfaces do not radiate heat well.

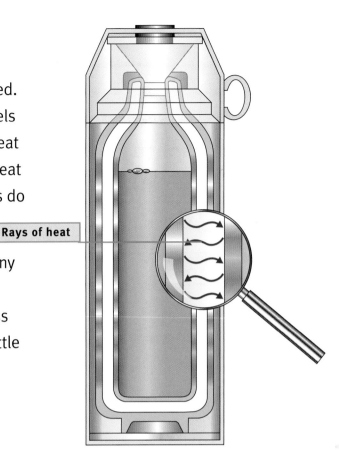

Rays of heat

As the gap between the glass walls does not have any air in it, heat cannot pass across it by conduction or convection. When the heat that does pass across the vacuum reaches the second shiny wall, very little is absorbed. A shiny surface is also very bad at absorbing heat. Most of the heat is reflected back to the first wall.

The movement of heat rays in the vacuum.

The very small amount of heat that is lost to the second glass wall then has another barrier to cross — the pieces of cork. Cork is a very good insulator and slows down the heat reaching the case. Insulators in the stopper slow down heat loss, too.

What made the temperature drop?

A thermos flask was filled with a hot drink and the temperature of the drink was taken every hour.

1 How much did the temperature change over the first three hours?

2 Why do you think the temperature had dropped so much after four hours?

3 Why did the temperature fall steadily again between 4 and 5 hours?

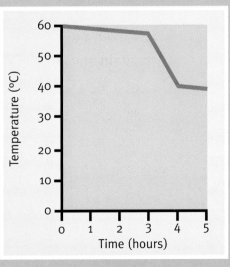

KEEPING HEAT OUT

We have seen that we use materials to keep heat in our bodies, our homes and our drinks. Materials can also be used to keep heat out of things, too.

insulating material

water from melted ice

The cotton wool acts as an insulator and stops the ice cube melting quickly.

Wrapping up an ice cube

If an ice cube is left in the open air, heat from the air enters it by conduction and the ice cube melts. When an insulating material, such as cotton wool, is wrapped around the ice cube the movement of heat is slowed down and the ice cube melts much more slowly.

Cool box

A cool box is used to keep foods cool for a picnic in summer. Its walls and lid are made of plastic which is a poor conductor and they also have air cavities in them. The air trapped in these cavities acts as an insulator too, making heat move very slowly into the box.

Cool boxes and bags keep drinks and food cool.

Liquid oxygen being poured from a flask. Some of it changes to gas as heat passes into it from the air.

Keeping things cool

The thermos flask was invented to keep heat out of a glass bottle. Warm air from outside the flask is prevented from going in and heating up the contents. This allows really cold substances, such as liquid oxygen, which has to be kept at a very low temperature, to be stored.

Reflecting a volcano's heat

Materials with a shiny surface reflect heat travelling as radiation. This scientist studying a volcano is wearing a shiny suit. The heat from the molten rocks is reflected away from the scientist's body so that it remains cool and safe.

Scientists sometimes need to take a close look at a volcano when it erupts.

Measuring in minus degrees

You may think that the coldest temperature is 0°C but it is not. Cold winter weather temperatures are measured in minus degrees. When you look at temperatures below 0°C, smaller numbers are warmer than larger numbers. For example, −10 is warmer than −15.

Arrange these temperatures in order starting with the warmest temperature:

−5°C, −34°C, −11°C, −59°C, −1°C

How many temperatures are below −11°C? Which ones are they?

CAN YOU REMEMBER THE ESSENTIALS?

Here are the essential science facts about keeping warm. They are set out in the order you can read about them in the book. Spend a couple of minutes learning each set of facts. If you can learn them all, you will know all the essentials about the science of keeping warm.

Heat and energy (pages 6–7)

Heat is a form of energy. Energy can change from one form to another form. The sun is a huge source of light and heat energy. Plants use some light energy from the sun to make food. Food contains stored chemical energy.

How heat moves (pages 10–11)

Heat always moves from a warmer place to a cooler place. Heat moves by conduction when two things are touching and one is warmer than the other. The flowing of liquids and gases carry heat by convection. Heat can travel as rays by radiation through space and the air.

Temperature (pages 8–9)

A thermometer is used to measure temperature. The coloured liquid in a thermometer is called alcohol. The Celsius and the Fahrenheit scales are used to measure temperature. Water freezes at 0°C or 32 °F and boils at 100°C or 212°F.

Conductors and insulators (pages 12–13)

A conductor allows heat to pass through it easily by conduction. An insulator does not let heat pass easily through it. Metals are good conductors. Wood, plastic, cork and cloth are insulators.

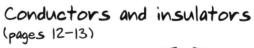

Body heat (pages 14–15)

When energy changes from one form to another, part of it always changes into heat.

When the energy in food changes, some of it becomes heat, which warms the body. Energy is released from food by a process called respiration. Oxygen is needed for respiration. Carbon dioxide is produced during respiration.

How animals keep warm (pages 20–21)

A cold-blooded animal cannot control its body temperature. A warm-blooded animal can keep its body temperature steady.

Cold-blooded animals use their muscles or the sun's rays to warm themselves up. Warm-blooded animals have a layer of insulation in their fur and feathers to keep them warm.

Sweating and shivering (pages 16–17)

The temperature at which our body works best and is most healthy is 37°C.

When we sweat the water in it evaporates and cools us down. The movement of muscles in shivering releases heat to warm us up.

People who get too hot suffer from heat stroke. People who get too cold suffer from hypothermia.

Keeping homes warm (pages 22–23)

Homes are warmed by electricity or fuels. Insulation helps to keep homes warm. Draught excluders stop heat escaping through gaps.

Double glazing reduces heat lost through windows. Cavity wall insulation reduces heat lost by walls. Insulation blankets in the roof space reduces heat lost through the roof.

Warm clothes (pages 18–19)

Warm clothes do not give us heat, they slow down heat leaving our bodies.

Warm clothes have fibres which trap air in spaces between them.

The air in warm clothes forms an insulating layer.

The thermos flask (pages 24–25)

Substances can be kept hot for a long time in a thermos flask.

The thermos flask has a vacuum cavity which stops heat moving by conduction and convection. The thermos flask has shiny walls which stop most heat moving by radiation. The thermos flask has parts made of cork and plastic which act as insulators.

Keeping heat out (pages 26–27)

Materials, which are used to keep heat in, can be used to keep heat out.

An insulating layer around an ice cube can help to keep it cool.

Shiny materials can reflect heat.

GLOSSARY

Birds Animals with a backbone and feathers that lay hard, shelled eggs.

Celsius scale A scale divided into 100 divisions called degrees Celsius.

Cold-blooded animal An animal that cannot keep its body temperature steady. Its temperature varies with the temperature of the surroundings.

Conduction The movement of heat as it spreads through a material or from one material to another.

Conductor A material which allows heat to pass through it quickly by conduction.

Convection The movement of heat as it is carried by a flowing liquid or gas.

Digest To break down food into very small particles so that it can be absorbed into the body.

Energy Something which allows an object or a living thing to take part in an activity. It may be moving or giving out light.

Evaporate To change from a liquid into a gas.

Experiments Investigations made to test observations and ideas.

Fahrenheit scale A scale divided into 212 divisions called degrees Fahrenheit.

Fibres Thin strands of material which may be long or short.

Fuel A material which is burnt to release heat energy.

Gravity The pulling force of attraction of a body, such as the Earth or the sun, upon objects at or near its surface.

Insect An animal without a backbone but with six legs and usually having either one or two pairs of wings.

Insulator A material which only allows heat to pass through it very, very slowly by conduction.

Irreversible change A change in which the materials taking part cannot be easily remade by a simple reversible change such as melting or freezing.

Mammals Animals with a backbone and hair which rear their young on milk for some time after they are born.

Metal A hard shiny material which conducts electricity.

Muscles Organs in the body which allow the parts of the body to move.

Photosynthesis A process in which plants make food from air, sunlight and water.

Plastic A solid material made from oil which does not conduct electricity, but which can burn or melt easily.

Radiation The movement of heat and light in the form of rays that can pass though air and space.

Reptile An animal with a backbone and a skin covered in scales which lays soft, shelled eggs.

Respiration The process in which living things release energy from food using oxygen and give out carbon dioxide and water.

Temperature The measure of the hotness or the coldness of something.

Thermograph A picture in which the colours represent different temperatures of the object.

Warm-blooded animals Animals which can keep their body temperature steady. It does not vary as the temperature of the surroundings change.

ANSWERS

Heat and energy (pages 6–7)
High-energy foods: spaghetti, peanut, chicken, bread, jam. Low-energy foods: apple, orange, milk, banana.

Temperature (pages 8–9)
The temperatures are A 10°C, B 22°C, C 40 °C.

How heat moves (pages 10–11)
The hottest parts are the flowing liquid and the base of the teapot. The coolest part are the handle of the teapot and the saucer.

Conductors and insulators (pages 12–13)
The best conductor is the copper spoon and the best insulator is the wooden spoon.

Body heat (pages 14–15)
1 Sleeping.
2 Soccer.
3 Activities in which the body only moves a little use small amounts of energy. Activities in which the body moves a great deal use a large amount of energy.
4 Sleeping, sitting at computer, walking, cycling, swimming, soccer.

Sweating and shivering (pages 16–17)
1 A 38°C, B 35.5 °C , C 37 °C, D 41.5 °C
2 B
3 D

Warm clothes (pages 18–19)
1 A 20°C, B 22 °C, C 19 °C, D 9 °C, E 32 °C, F 25 °C
2 D
3 E

How animals keep warm (pages 20–21)
1 Rattlesnake.
2 Pigeon, dog.
3 Rattlesnake.

Keeping homes warm (pages 22–23)
1 9%
2 5%
3 23%
4 20%

The thermos flask (pages 24–25)
1 About 3 °C.
2 Someone had removed the stopper.
3 Someone had put the stopper back on.

Keeping heat out (pages 26–27)
1 –1°C, –5°C, –11°C, –34°C, –59°C
2 Two, –34°C, –59°C

INDEX